For Richard & Mark & Hugo

ISBN: 0-9677003-0-2

Published by Edwina Sandys
565 Broadway, New York, NY 10012
(1-800-566-6630)
www.edwinasandys.com
Printed by Dollco Printing in Canada

First edition

EVE & ADAM
by
Edwina Sandys

"The Book of Life begins with a man and a woman in a garden. It ends with revelations."

Oscar Wilde

Eve & Adam
in the
Garden of Eden

A week is a long time in politics. It was an eternity in the Garden of Eden. God made heaven and earth in the short space of seven days. Last of his work, but not least, was the creation of Man – and Woman. Actually Woman was created before Man!

Human embryos, when first formed, are all female. Later, some of them develop male characteristics – the female X chromosome drops a "leg" and becomes a Y. So, you can see in those early days, Adam was definitely missing something.

What Adam was missing was curiosity. It was no accident that it was Eve, the lively, outgoing and curious one, not Adam, who was chatted up by the serpent in the Garden of Eden.

When Eve took that first bite of the fruit of the Tree of Knowledge, she became a changed person. Eve was already formed with a brain – the hardware. But with the Apple of Knowledge installed, she now had the software to run it. An irreversible process had taken place.

From this point on, throughout history, Eve's actions have been misinterpreted. Her dilemma: should she keep this new "knowledge" for herself – or should she share it with Adam? Keeping it for herself, she would reign supreme, and Adam would be her servant – an unquestioning simpleton. But not to invite Adam to enjoy the exciting new opportunities that lay ahead, on equal terms with her, would be selfish.

As we all know, Eve did share her "knowledge" with Adam. And this gift of intelligence, combined with man's innate superior physical strength, enable Adam to subjugate Eve. By this simple act of generosity, Eve gave Adam her proxy vote in the shaping of the future.

Exiled from the Garden of Eden for eating the forbidden fruit, Eve follows Adam into Modern Times – and then we don't hear much from her for millions of years to come.

Edwina Sandys

In the beginning God
created the heaven and
the earth. And the earth
was without form, and
void; and darkness was
upon the face of the
deep.

Genesis I

The Void

And God formed woman
of the dust of the ground,
and breathed into her
nostrils the breath of life;
and woman became a
living soul.

Genesis I

Creation of Eve

And the hip, which the Lord
God had taken from
woman, made he a man.
And Eve said: he shall
be called Man, because
he was taken out of
Woman.

Genesis 2

Birth of Adam

And they were both naked, the woman and her husband, and were not ashamed.

Genesis 2

Innocence

And God commanded them, saying; Of every tree of the garden thou mayest freely eat; But of the Tree of Knowledge of Good and Evil, thou shalt not eat of it or thou shalt surely die.

Genesis 2.

Forbidden Fruit

Now the serpent was more subtle than any beast of the field and said unto the woman, "Ye shall not surely die, for God doth know that in the day ye eat thereof, then your eyes shall be opened and ye shall be as gods.

Genesis 3

Curiosity

And when the woman saw
that the tree was good for
food, and that it was
pleasant to the eyes, and
a tree to be desired to make
one wise, she took of the
fruit thereof, and did
eat.

Genesis 3

Original Sin

And her eyes were opened.

Genesis 3

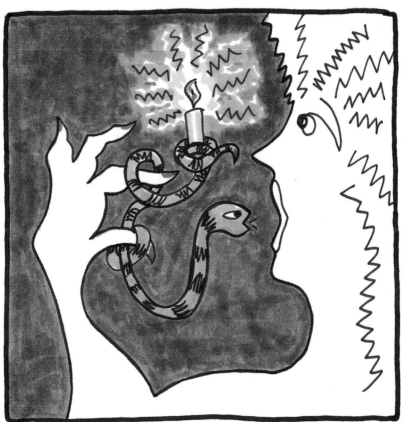

Enlightenment

And she gave also unto her husband, and he did eat.

Genesis 3

Temptation

And Eve knew Adam
her husband.

Genesis 4

Carnal Knowledge

They knew that they were
naked; and they sewed
fig leaves together, and
made themselves aprons.

Genesis 3

Cover Up

And they heard the voice of God walking in the garden in the cool of the day, and Eve and her husband hid themselves ... And God saith unto the woman, "What is this that thou hast done?... I will greatly multiply thy sorrow and thy conception: And thy desire shall be to thy husband, and he shall rule over thee.

Genesis 4

Shame

And the Lord God said,
"Behold, the woman is
become as one of us, to
know good and evil; and
now, lest she put forth
her hand, and take also
of the Tree of Life and
eat, and live for ever,
therefore do I send them
forth from the Garden
of Eden.

Genesis 3

Expulsion

Adam & Eve
in Modern Times

Banished from the Garden of Eden, Adam leads Eve
into Modern Times.

Following God's instructions, they go forth and multiply.
They "beget" and "begat" until the world has "begotten"
billions.

Adam also obeyed God's mandate to subdue the earth
and "have dominion over every living thing." Adam rules.

Adam and Eve flock to the big cities and lose touch with
nature. Cooped up in little boxes in the sky, they
communicate with other people electronically. Everything
can be ordered on the internet. The only people who need
to emerge are singles when they're looking for sex. And
they daren't leave home without a plastic wrapper.

In this confusing world, Adam and Eve search for God.
Where is He? Who is He? He's no longer that old
gentleman up there with the flowing white beard.
Is He a he? Is there a There, there?

Be ye fruitful and multiply.

Genesis 6

Population when unchecked, increases in a geometrical ratio.

Thomas Robert Malthus

One child per family.

Chairman Mao

One of the best things people could do for their descendants would be to sharply limit their numbers.

Olin Miller

Population: Explosion

Therefore is the name of the
city called Babel; because
the Lord did there confound
the language of all the earth.

Genesis II

God made the country and
man made the town.

J. H. Payn

We shape our buildings.
Thereafter they shape us.

Winston S. Churchill

It's not a concrete jungle,
it's a human zoo.

Desmond Morris

Home Sweet Home

What hath God wrought?

Numbers 6

Quoted by Samuel Morse in the
first electric message ~ 1844

Man is still the greatest
computer of all.

John F. Kennedy

Computers are useless. They
can only give you answers.

Pablo Picasso

Reach Out and Touch Someone

Give me chastity and continence,
but not just now.

St. Augustine

An ounce of prevention is
better than a pound of cure.

Proverb

You're not just sleeping with
one person, you're sleeping with
everyone they ever slept with.

Theresa Crenshaw

Life is a sexually transmitted
disease.

Guy Bellamy

Safe Sex

I wouldn't put it past God to arrange a virgin birth, but I very much doubt if he would. David Jenkins (Bishop of Durham)

Hello Dolly!

Newspaper headlines on the birth of the first cloned sheep.

In vitro vanitas. Anon

Immaculate Conception

Marriage is for the procreation
of children.

The Bible

I've noticed that everyone
that is for abortion has
already been born.

Ronald Reagan

If men could get pregnant,
abortion would be a
sacrament.

Florynce Kennedy

Family Planning

What God hath joined
together, let not Man put
asunder. St. Matthew 19

Home life is no more
natural to us than a cage
is natural to a cockatoo.
George Bernard Shaw

Paying alimony is like
feeding hay to a dead
horse. Groucho Marx

'Til Death Us Do Part

The spirit indeed is willing but the flesh is weak.
St. Matthew 26

Imprisoned in every fat man, a thin one is wildly signalling to be let out. Cyril Connally

Nothing succeeds like excess. Oscar Wilde

Food for Thought

Vanity of vanities, all is vanity.

Ecclesiastes I

A sound body means a sound mind.

Juvenal

Stay young and beautiful
It's your duty to be beautiful

1950's song for BBC
Woman's Hour

Body Beautiful

The fashion of this world
passeth away.

Corinthians I

There's only one thing...
worse than being talked
about, and that is not
being talked about

Oscar Wilde

We're more popular than
Jesus Christ now.

John Lennon

In the future everyone
will be famous for fifteen
minutes.

Andy Warhol

Role Model

In my name shall they cast out devils.

St. Mark

Psychiatry enables us to correct our faults by confessing our parents' shortcomings.

Laurence J. Peter

A psychiatrist is a man who goes to The Folies Bergères and looks at the audience.

Mervyn Stockwood (Bishop of Southwark)

Sometimes a cigar is just a cigar.

Sigmund Freud

The Shrink

Get thee behind me, Satan.
St. Mark

Folks who have no vices
have very few virtues.
Abraham Lincoln

Let's find out what
everyone is doing. And
then stop everyone from
doing it.   A.P. Herbert

It's all right to drink like
a fish ~ if you drink what
a fish drinks.
Mary Pettibone Poole

Just say No

Touch not, taste not, handle not.
St. Paul

The testimony of a woman
has only half the value
of the testimony of a man.
Ancient Law

When woman say "No"
she mean "Yes".
Calypso Song

Sexual Harassment

Wine maketh merry, but money answereth all things.

Ecclesiastes I

If you really want to make a million, the quickest way is to start your own religion.

L. Ron Hubbard

Money... was exactly like sex, you thought of nothing else if you didn't have it, and thought of other things if you did.

James Baldwin

Money is better than poverty, if only for financial reasons.

Woody Allen

The Root of All Evil

Thou shalt not make unto thee
any graven image.   Exdus

He knows all about art but he
doesn't know what he likes.
                    James Thurber

Anyone who paints a sky green
and pastures blue ought to be
sterilized.
                    Adolph Hitler

Art is not a pastime but a
Priesthood.   Jean Cocteau

The new job of art is to sit
on the wall and get more
expensive.
                    Robert Hughes

Art for Art's Sake

And the Lord God said ...
replenish the earth and subdue
it. Have dominion over the
fish of the sea, and over the
fowl of the air, and over every
living thing that moveth upon
the earth.   Genesis 7

Après nous le déluge.

Madame de Pompadour

It's hard for me to get
used to these changing times.
I can remember when the
air was clean and sex was
dirty.   George Burns

Global warning

A time of war, and a time of peace.
Ecclesiastes 8

We turned the switch, saw the flashes,
confirming that the atom could be
split. That night I knew the
world was headed for sorrow.
Leo Szilard ~ 1939

The atomic bomb is the Second Coming
in wrath.
Winston S. Churchill

People want peace so badly, governments
ought to get out of their way and let
them have it. Dwight D. Eisenhower

We'll all go together when we go.
Tom Lehrer

Nuclear Deterrent

Canst thou by searching
find out God?

Job 11

Hope springs eternal in
the human breast.

Alexander Pope

If God did not exist, it would
be necessary to invent him.

Voltaire

There are no atheists in the foxholes.

William Thomas Cummings ~ 1943

There's no "there" there. Gertrude Stein

Listen: there's a hell of a good universe
next door; let's go.

e.e. cummings

The One God

The New Millennium

God's prediction in the Garden of Eden has come true. Adam and Eve have challenged his rule. They, themselves, have become mini-gods and, for the first time in history, have the power to turn the lights off.

God has put up with the adventures of Eve and Adam from the beginning of time to the brink of chaos. Will he ever put his foot down?

I am Alpha and Omega, the beginning and the ending, saith the Lord, which is and which was, and which is to come.

Revelations I

...and the sun became black as sackcloth of hair, and the moon became as blood; And the stars of heaven fell unto earth, even as a fig tree casteth her untimely figs when she is shaken of a mighty wind.

For the great day of his wrath is come; and who shall be able to stand?

Revelations 7

Judgement Day

For, behold, I create new heavens and a new earth; and the former shall not be remembered, nor come into mind.

But be ye glad and rejoice for ever in that which I create:

I will bring forth a seed... an inheritor of my mountains: and mine elect shall inherit it.

Isaiah 26

Starting Over

What's past is prologue.

Shakespeare

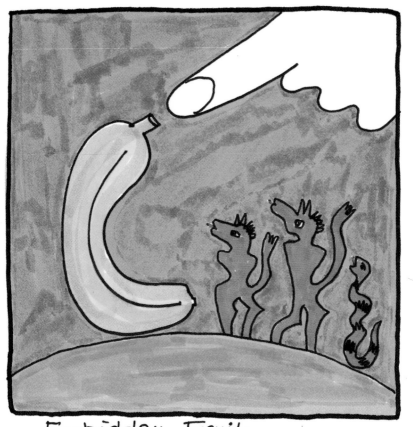

Forbidden Fruit

Que Sera . . . . . .